THE DAYS I DREAM OF

Chardonnay

First Edition

3 5 7 9 10 8 6 4 2

Saint John's, Antigua
West Indies

ISBN: 9798223893202

Images from Canva ©

Visit the author's website at
https://lmsanguinette.wordpress.com

DEDICATION

This book of poems is dedicated to my sister, the kindest woman I know—especially after a glass of wine.

"It is time to bask in the depths of curiosity, swim in the oceans of critical thought, down the last drop of wine."
~L. M. Sanguinette

THE DAYS I DREAM OF

Chardonnay

A COLLECTION OF POEMS

L. M. Sanguinette

CONTENTS

ACKNOWLEDGMENTS

I'd like to thank all those who have been following along on my curious writing journey. Specifically, the teachers who nurtured my creativity back in high school, where most of these poems originated. Although there have been many modifications since—thankfully—and my writing style has improved over the years, I would be remiss not to attribute part of my success to these wonderful people. These teachers were the ones who cultivated my love of poetry and allowed it to grow into what it is today.

The next stroke of gratitude goes out to an icon of the genre, Shel Silverstein. To those of you who have never read the genius that is Shel Silverstein, I do in fact pity you, for your imaginations were never blessed with such images of crocodiles at dental appointments, empty house heads, sister auctions, and more. His poems were my first introduction to the wonderful world of poetry and to this day still serve as inspiration for my works.

In addition to the two previous acknowledgements, I'd like to thank my editor Cara Flannery of Fluky Fiction. She has been my guiding light on this journey, and I will continue to thank her from now until the end of time for all that she has helped me with and all that she continues to do.

Next, I'd like to thank my friends Jade, Emma, Tiffany, Rachele, Sara, and Megan who serve as the inspiration for some of these poems. These girls consistently see me through my darkest moments, offering to lend an ear over a cup of coffee, a chocolate ice cream, and when necessary, a bottle (or two) of chardonnay. I do not know where I would be without their encouragement.

Moving on, I'd like to thank my cousin Quin Farara for helping me with the wine-related trivia. I am definitely not a connoisseur—though I know enough to enjoy the good and avoid the bad—so I am glad to have one in the family. I am not the kind of person who dances around issues, though I do tend to jump straight to the point without giving adequate context, so thank you again for answering most of my rather obscure and seemingly out-of-nowhere questions. He probably won't realize that he is mentioned in this, but it'll make for a good conversation when he decides he's ready to pick up a copy.

Finally, as always, I'd like to thank my family for all their support: my parents, who have always wanted the best for me, even though my career path has taken an unexpected turn (in their eyes); my siblings, who constantly keep me on my toes and bring a smile to my face; and my partner, who puts up with all my nonsense. I love you guys.

INTRODUCTION

This is the third instalment in the **Days I Dream** series, preceded by *The Days I Dream of Chocolate* and *The Days I Dream of Coffee*.

This collection is somewhat more light-hearted and fantastical than the others as it was influenced by the titular subject. I never intended to follow through with the alliterative nomenclature, but I must admit it has a ring to it as a series. The poems in this collection were designed to be enjoyed with a tall glass of wine and a very open mind. Each of the five sections contains poems of a different theme following the taste profile of each wine: Sauternes being sweet, Sancerre tart, Provence Rose silky, Chardonnay bold, and Bordeaux traditional.

This collection is comprised of experiences in the form of poems, some of which are my own and others are simply evocatively fictitious experiences. My goal with this collection is to provide snippets of experiences that spark the imagination of you the reader and leave you feeling as satisfied as if you'd finished the corresponding bottle.

SAUTERNES

Starting off sweet and sumptuous, Sauternes is a French sweet wine originating in Bordeaux and made from Sémillon, Sauvignon Blanc, and muscadelle grapes that have been affected by noble rot. Sauternes are some of the longest-lived wines, typically starting out golden yellow and growing darker with age, reaching more matured and complex flavours, until it reaches the colour of an old copper coin.

Characterized by the balance of sweetness and acidity, some common Sauternes flavour notes include apricots, honey, peaches, and nuttiness, with a finish that lingers on the palate well past the final sip.

Enjoy a glass of this sweet wine chilled at 10°C (50°F), paired with a nice foie gras, goat cheese, and the following poems of joy and childlike wonder.

WAKING UP WITH THE SUN

my youthful eyes knew only life
as the morning sun crept in,
the early hours of dawn beckoning
a new adventure to begin.

BEFORE I KNEW OF GETTING OLD

i wore robes of leaf and crowns of twig
and lived in palaces of stone
collected from the many shores
of oceans i'd never travelled
but waded into on a whim
thinking myself a siren strong
whose song could heal a sailor's heart
before I knew of getting old.

PIGTAILS AND PLASTERS

the days were longer then, or i was smaller too,
when i wore pigtails and a uniform to school
and roamed around the playground
without a care in the world
the days stretched on
the months became years
the years became decades
in the mind of a child
back when i brandished
plasters on my knees
from running and falling
rather than on my heels
from standing and walking.

CHILDHOOD MEMORIES

if i could go back and waste away
the days to chasing butterflies
and pretending that the fireflies
were wishing stars watched by childish eyes,
i might just lose myself in the wish
that there were nothing to reminisce,
for that present, present gifted
and daydreams made and spirits lifted,
where nothing mourned and nothing lost
and joy endured and responsibility naught.
fondest are the memories
that roam my mind eternally
as tethered ground may be dismissed
imagination, ignorant bliss.

ON DAYS LIKE TODAY

on days like today, i stare at the clouds
wondering how high i'd have to jump
to hit my head on the ceiling—
their ceiling, my floor.

as i stare into space, it begins to take shape
that cinema in the sky whose tales unfold
where lands warp and animals race
and a whale swallows the sun.

i'll think to myself, as i watch them go by
from my double-glazed window,
four stories high in the office
where i am not me but a number
and summertime sadness creeps in.

AFTERWORK THOUGHTS

again, i toss myself on the couch
after a long day of little work
of doing things i know
a machine would do better,
things that were made
to give reason to my being,
that being were not reason enough.

again, they prod for work to be done
which needs little doing but must look like a lot
for they need to pay a someone
and not a something
which works out best for me
seeing as i need to sustain
my curling up on the couch.

KING OF THE SKIES

the sun and i have made a bargain
i've promised away my laughter and smiles
in exchange for his kindness and care.

he watches over me in wait
for the day that i return to him
my humble king of the skies.

ESPERANZA

my body is the home of hope
my temple Esperanza
housing dreams and fantasies
that shall not be ignored
or forgotten.

PEBBLE IN THE SAND

i am nothing but a pebble
stuck between land and sea
tumbling down banks and shores
whose waves remind me of what i'm missing
pulling me forward towards the unknown
but whose sands hold fast and hold tight
fears and doubts and duties and past
all praying i stay the same.

GRAPE VINES AND BOOK SPINES

i follow the tales of heroes and kings
on journeys that curve like grapevines
across inked pages and broken spines
well into the dark of night.

i root for the romance i find on shelves
of bookstores and libraries alike
falling in love with fictional men
that have no chance of falling for me.

i get lost in the dreams and fantasies
that take up residency in my mind
a haven to escape from reality
where i can bask in happier ends.

MANY A BALLAD

i pray that one day this tale finds you
well and good and you realize
that many years have passed since
but your heart still rings
in the back of my mind.

many a ballad have i written
to eyes who will never see
and ears who will never hear
for poetry and patience
were never your suits of choice.

BREAK IN THE STORM

storm clouds were once a sign of sadness
'til it dawned on me that they were veils
curtains masking only happiness
if only i could cast off the grey.

a storm lasts but a moment
the thunder echoes but echoes alone
i realized the sun was only hiding
saving its beauty for that break in the storm.

SUNLIGHT THROUGH OFFICE WINDOWS

i am a daydreamer by nature—
or so i say to those worried my hand will slip
from beneath the point of my chin as i gaze
unfazed through the windows of my latest cage.

in my mind, i am miles away—worlds away.

i am the heroine with the broadsword
who dethrones the wicked king
and rides on the backs of scaly dragons
into the twilight sky.

as my eyes follow the outlines of the mountains
whose freedom mocks me at my desk
and whose grasses gleam a brighter green
than any picture on my screen.

i am not quite here nor there.

a haze floods my mind, but not before
i question if it is you standing across from me
with the quizzical brow and worried lip tremor
at my unresponsive daze.

or if, like my missing dragon,
you are a figment of another world,
one that will slip from view
when sounds the next zoom call.

it's okay, i say, i am a daydreamer by nature.

CHILDISH SMILE

long have you admired that twinkle in my eyes,
that fire you claim is spontaneity—or alike.
long have you gazed in awe as i dance around rooms
listening to tunes that only my mind can hear,
hoping that one day, they'd rub off on you, too.

i've watched your stares and quizzical brows,
i know you wish you could grow down as i have,
to embrace the savage, the wild and free
that you have long since learned to ignore
in order to adhere to 'better nature.'

but nature is the name of my game,
and one you've come to realize may seem like
a calculated childishness by the strength of my smile,
but rather stems from a truth i hold inside
that keeps my spirit young and sweet.

for i will not play by the rules laid out
but seek the path of joy innate
which may seem childish to those who cannot see
the beauty in being and living and loving
and to those who find fault in my childish smile.

CHARDONNAY

Chardonnay is a wine known for its great complexity and versatility, with a wide range of flavour notes, such as tropical fruits, citrus, and apple, as well as buttery and nutty aromas derived from oak aging. On the palate, Chardonnay can be crisp and refreshing, or rich and creamy, with flavors that can range from green apple and lemon to vanilla and toasted hazelnut.

Like a well-crafted sonnet, Chardonnay balances structure and beauty with acidity and age. The best Chardonnays are made with care and attention to detail, leaving a finished product that is complex, layered, and elegant.

To fully appreciate Chardonnay, serve it chilled at 10-12°C (50-54°F) and pair it with rich and flavorful dishes and the subsequent poems. As you sip, let the wine inspire you to write your own sonnet, exploring the beauty and complexity of the world around you.

THE JOURNEY TO THE END

it is a journey to be sure
growing up and growing older
one i'd wished for but never sought to find
the fool's gold in the promised chest
with no way back to the cherished start
and a final destination we are taught to fear.

but i am learning to stall the clock
to cling to imagination and relish in dreams
and remind myself of the childhood past
in spite of the schedules that chain me to the future
and the voices that demand i fall in line
for i am along for the journey.

SAVED BY VERSE

i could've given in to the voices in my head
or the fear in my heart or the pain in my chest
over things i cannot control or change.

i could've cried an ocean of tears
listening to comments i'd rather not hear
from people who don't quite see me.

i could've fallen prey to society's games
that ask that i give all and then some
in exchange for a dream i never desired.

I could've, but I was saved by verse.

WALKING ON GLASS

i'd never known how to swim on land
until i was left to drown alone
by the one who'd once promised
to save me from rainy days
but instead stole my umbrella.
now i tiptoe across fields of glass
owned by the one who i thought
would protect me from splinters
would be my safe haven
and who now asks why
my breathing is shallow
why my heart is weak
why my eyes are red
like the blood on my feet
that hides the damage of his shards.

DIMMED STARS

the world around me smiles
the world inside me breaks
the stress of it all became too much
my eyes burn, my heart aches.

i was made to dim my light
to dowse the star within
for hollow people who feared my warmth
against their paper skin.

i was made to believe i was too much
and somehow never enough
i lost the parts of me i loved
to those who wanted my lust.

But time has taught me not to fear
to shine the way I know best
that whosoever I burn in the process
was never meant to pass its test.

AUTOMATON

I am not a machine, *I say*
but the voices in my head say different. Day in, day out, on
automation. Little girl be patient.
I am not a machine... *I repeat with less conviction 'til the*
words begin to fade and string and slur together.
I am not a machine...
I amnot a machine...
am not amachine...
Aim not a machine...
Maybe take a break, they say, and you'll be fixed another day,
ai m not a machine...
Iam not a cchamine...
Iam not a chanmeine...
Machine iam no...
I am not a mahine...
Aiem not am chamine...
With little pockets of consciousness I scream,
Am not a machine! *But a new day brings a new haze and*
judgment wanes like the moon above.
Iam not a ma chine...
I am not a mavhine...
I am boe t a mavhine...
I am not. Am achine...
Oa m not ma amachine...
And down I descend to the maddening depths of monotony,
where conscious thought has left me, completely.
Ia fewbot a macbieb...
Iamf abont a machine...
I am not am ahcine...
I amfrbo ta mavhine...

I amg noy a mavhciene…
Ia mnot a mahcien…
I amno ta mahvine…
I ma ot. Qam achine…
I am not am ahine…
Until I'm drained of coffee and after months of good nights'
sleep, I stare back at the string of days that all blend in to one
and think, am not I a machine?

I wasn't built, I was born.
I wasn't bred, I was nurtured.
I am not the product of blueprint and binding.
I am not to be measured by a single failure or faulty wire.
I am not perfect, nor was I meant to be…
I am not a machine.

THE SMALLER THE STAKES

I was never contented with
the simple life
the nine to five
the house on the hill
the working for the weekend
'cause that system never worked.

Why retire if I am inspired
by the fantasies that make my mind
ageless?

Who's to say?
I might live better that way
if I followed the grain
and learned to be okay
sent my dreams down the drain
like the dirt on my shower floor…

But smaller stakes did no bonfire make
and if my bet should burn,
let it blaze.

I have contented myself with
this new kind of torture
the bending over backwards
to the sounds of the masters that
live rent free in my mind,
the ones who watch on as I jot down
their stories as seen through my eyes.

I could turn away—I should turn away
but their voices hark louder than any siren's song.

I must fight, I must write,
I can't quit 'til the stories are gone.
If this is never, then all for the better
to be writing with one foot in the grave.

My life could be easy,
maybe even sweet
if I allowed myself to breathe
and be pleased with not being seen
but I know the me I'm meant to be
wasn't made for smaller stakes.

I LIVE TO PLEASE

I'm sorry if my words are not polished and pristine
Or if my voice may seem hollow and cold
But I am long since done with my need to please
I've abandoned everything I'd once known.

At home, I grew up needing to be seen
But being seen doing all that was right
In the eyes of those who couldn't hold my hands
Because my edges were too sharp, my light, too bright.

My little smart mouth said as was wanted
But at what cost to my sanity?
I'd moulded myself into the best for all,
I'll make you happy, make you proud, then I'll be
happy, too… maybe…

Satisfaction was the game and perfect was my aim
But then I woke up in a house filled with trinkets
And things I don't know if I've ever liked
And a job in a place that the little me hates
And a lack of time and a lot of memories that
I could let go of for they don't feel like mine at all.

I've reached the end of a missing childhood
and wish nothing more than to go back
and discover the real me and my wants and my needs
rather than find them at the bottom of this bottle
that I now sip on because I am 'grown.'

The wine is gone, the bottle remains
full of remorse and regret
for the life I lived to please and which
I discarded the day I grew up.

DISCONNECTED

a shame that only two feet away
we stare at screens that make it seem
as though we were face-to-face.

we type away as if to say
we miss the sound of each other's voice
but our bodies speak a different tongue.

our laughs are shared
through faces with no bodies
while we wear blank eyes and slack jaws.

it was never before this way
but this disease extends
nowadays to even the children.

this play at personability
is just as pretend as it was
back when we held rocks in place of phones.

but now, the silent treatment is expected
and not writing is a louder message
and we all curse the blessing of
being disconnected.

HELLO ANXIETY, MY OLD FRIEND

nobody told me that these demons would stay
that they'd poison my mind,
worse now than before.

that they'd eat away at what little remained
of my sane heart and gentle core.

that i'd war with myself over trivial things
like what i said or what i wore
or what i did or ate.

nobody told me that i'd learn to hate
criticize myself like i were not me but mistake
tear myself down the way no other would, or should,
and break and break and break.

i am but an hourglass, toiling away
as the polished crystal filter, but a shell
for the rawness i hold within,
a drop away from shattering.

hello Anxiety, my old friend.
i see you still accompany me
though you too have grown.

Is it I or the wine that has made space for you?

THE TICKING OF THE CLOCK

Racing against the ticking clock
that beats inside my chest,
the one that says there's more to do
and will not let me rest.

My goals and dreams are not yet achieved
the voice in my head screams don't quit,
this is not why you are here, my dear,
don't settle, this isn't it.

By the ticking of the clock
and the pricking of my thumbs
I won't let the days all waste away
nor let them blur into one.

By the ticking of the clock
whose steady beat keeps my time
I am a body, I am a soul
I am a dreamer divine.

By the beating of my heart
its timbre like a drum
let not my feet walk in agony
let not my mind go numb.

And were I to shun the clock inside
I might find myself freed
but the tick and tock of the ticking clock
are the calls which I must heed.

And so I follow the ticking clock
I shall not rest or sit
painful in my praised torture
in purpose's poisoned pit.

BROKEN ARE THE FILTERS

a shame no one looks at a rose for its beauty
but rather to capture a moment made false
by the filters and fictitious captions
that frequent a 'fairytale' life.

where capture gives reason to conversations paid
to sell the illusion of a contemplation that never was.
for a picture may be worth a thousand words
but a moment made is always priceless.

and priced less are the times that should be regarded
those we will no longer get back, for there is no back
though many springs may sprout new roses
a moment lost is lost forever.

TANTRUMS

i once thought—or was convinced by the world—
only children threw tantrums when they got upset
tear-stained cheeks and little red noses
eyes that glaze over, helpless and distraught
kicking and screaming for all to see.

What I've since then learned is
I throw them too, discreet but deranged
in bathroom stalls and powder rooms
and behind closed doors, where
no one can see or hear or help.

FIGURE YOUR SH*T OUT

step up your game
get it right
get up early
be on time
watch your health
stop daydreaming
do better—be better
your train is leaving
brush the sleep from your eyes
learn your place
fall in line
break your back to please the rest
sweep your dreams under the bed
—haven't you heard? dreams are dead—
business doesn't ever sleep
don't let laziness set
don't sit
don't slouch
don't ever forget
hold your tongue
cool your bones
be the person we expect
leave the fantasies alone
find yourself a better home
don't become the one we reject
you'll never be perfect
but you still have to try
push and push until you die
you've got nothing to cry about
—get the message yet? figure your shit out!

MY LIFE ON THE LINE

they say i'm crazy
a little bit ballsy to move from the city
that learned me, that taught me
but i've got no time to be wasting
and i'm tired of being patient
with people who see not my struggle or story
and watch me with eyes hungry for my glory

it's boring
when they're fighting just a little
and i'm warring like i'm dying
but it's my turf and my turn
and my life on the line
and though it still hurts
i've got no time for crying

i'm trying
my eyes are red, but tears won't fall
i'm stronger than this, stronger than it all
i've climbed the mountains and broken the walls
they once put up to hold me, to cage me
giving me limits thinking they'd stay me
putting up roadblocks in hopes that they'd sway me

but i wasn't lazy
or built to be caged
and i'm not living my life like a play on a stage
with a curtain that isn't mine to close
because that wasn't the life i chose
it's my life on the line, and that's not going to change
so get up or get out but don't stand in my way.

NOTHING LINGERS…

They smile their soft smiles as I drown my sorrows,
another glass to help dull the pains of tomorrow.

But nothing lingers they say, and I groan,
if only they'd known, if only they'd known.

The scent of pine fades from the dangling car tree,
which is why cab drivers use two or three.

The sting of failed tests lasts only a while,
not even the teachers keep those kinds of files.

The fresh feel of a new car, a new house, new clothes.
Even those too will eventually grow old.

The bitter taste of bad coffee and lingering bad breath.
But that too will fade, as will mourning a death.

It's true what they say that nothing lingers forever,
but, oh, how I know it gets worse before better.

They try to console me, set my thoughts adrift
They say nothing lingers like a fart in a lift…

So, I laugh, how I laugh, choke back sobs as I think
there's nothing that lingers quite like that stink.

Not mourning, not sweet scents,
not new clothes or bad breath.
Not bitter coffee, not heartbreak
not deep cuts or death.

Be it rationale or drunken haze, I haven't a clue,
there's one thing my mind now seems to hold true:

All things fade, all bad things but this,
because nothing lingers like a fart in a lift.

SANCERRE

Sancerre is a crisp, tart white wine hailing from the Loire Valley. Made from the Sauvignon Blanc grape, this wine is known for its bright acidity and refreshing citrus flavors, like lemon, grapefruit, and lime, as well as hints of minerals, thanks to the chalky soils in which it is grown.

Sancerre balances acidity and texture with precision, resulting in a wine that is both refreshing and elegant. As the wine warms in the glass, it opens up to reveal layers of flavor. The finish is long and lingering, like the final lines of a poem that stays with you long after it's been read.

For the ultimate experience, serve Sancerre chilled at 8-10°C (46-50°F) and let the tartness of the wine inspire your own verses of a tart nature.

WHO KILLED IMAGINATION?

no more do we talk about treehouses
as if they were castles floating on clouds.

no longer are we the kings and queens
of the fortresses we built out of sofa cushions.

gone are the days we would play in the dirt
and cook up banquets made for only the worms.

lost are the times we could stare at the sky
and convince ourselves that the sun shone for us.

Because someone has killed imagination.

somewhere between twelve and thirteen
we saw the signs of sickness set in.

the illness that the world convinced us of curing
the childish fantasies in our minds has festered.

leaving us with nothing but the nine-to-five
we never wanted but were made to believe we did.

where the plan is to retire to do what we love
because nothing we did before was good enough.

Because someone has killed imagination.

IF I WERE A BETTER GIRL

if i were a better girl,
i might have wished to change the world
might have prayed to god above
to fix the lonely broken hearts
to heal the hurting and the poor
might have let the livestock loose
and found a reason for no war
i could've help the many migrants
whose houses were destroyed
gotten rid of all the poachers
or reign in corrupted kings
handed out a stipend so
that none would ever need
i might have brought about world peace
or ridden us of hunger too
i could've changed the politics
and cured the worst disease
i could've made it so no child
would ever need to bleed
i could've, should've, would've
if that could've could've been…
but the world told me i wasn't her.
she wasn't me.
I'm not that better girl.

WHY DID YOU BREAK THE MIRROR?

bracing for another day
of tiresome work and little play
wondering if the wine tonight
will make me happy or make me fight
and thinking back on the child whose dreams
included none of these adulting scenes
but rather pixies and mermaids and fairytale ends
in far-off places with animal friends…

so i ask the woman in the bathroom mirror
who thinks mostly of gym time and cooking dinner
and prays for the bottle at the end of the day
and has no time for fantasy or childish play
if she misses the girl she used to be
the one that laughed and lived carefree
but the woman reflected only shakes her head
saying *time took her and left me instead.*

That's why I broke the mirror.

AM I TOO MUCH?

there are times when i wonder

if my voice is too loud
if my smile is too proud
if the stomp of my boots
leaves tremors in the ground
if my eyes are too bright
if my hugs are too tight
if the tone of my speech
doesn't sound all that right…

throughout the years
i'd boxed myself in
cut my tongue
changed my grin
faded into the background
of the many bright stars
i couldn't but wished to be
in theory i've broken free

and yet i still question
the sway of my walk
the way that i talk
the clothes that I wear
the sweep of my hair
the force of my glare
the essence of my soul
the break in my whole

Still, I wonder, am I too much?

DISSOCIATION

Again, it kicks in
over a glass of wine
as I dine with friends that
I'm sure are real, corporeal at least,
but question all the same…

i wonder if i myself exist
if me as a person should at this time
in this world with one sun and one moon
was i truly made for this?
made for anything at all?

where would i be otherwise?
who would i be?
what would i do?
what would i see?
how did i end up here instead?

The wine doesn't hurt
but it doesn't help either
with the crisis-non-crisis
that plagues my mind
infrequently, and all on its own.

Another sip will bring me back
away from the torture
that never stops, only sleeps
waiting for another day
in which to question a lifetime.

JO MALONE ON CHRISTMAS

You fell first but I fell hard
for the idea of what could be
but you weren't there to catch it
when my heart decided to leap.

I played it cool and played it coy
a mouse and cat, like in days of old
but no one told me of your games
how it was cat and toy.

Further still, fell I for the trap
for the seduction in your fiery eyes
for the words I misinterpreted
to be more than banter and tease.

I convinced myself that I was it
the end goal and the dream
but stone-cold hearts will never break
when cages are built with no doors.

It's like Jo Malone on Christmas
under a New York City tree
the pretty package, a luring sight
with the promise of something sweet.

Until I realized time was the master
of games I was never meant to beat
because time will turn perfume to poison
and your vacant heart poisoned me.

THE SOCK UNDER THE BED

I lost myself.
The person I thought I was.
The person I wanted to be.
Somewhere between
learning to live and living
I lost myself,
I forgot myself.
I became the sock under the bed.

SWEET WORDS NO CANDY MADE

I refuse to sour my lips with
the poisoned honey that leaches from
mouths whose hearts were long scorned
and left to settle scores with
the ghosts of lovers past.

SWEET WORDS NO CANDY MADE

I refuse to sour my lips with
the poisoned honey that leaches from

WARRING WATERS

I wage my wars in silence
because I've learned how not to speak
to those whose ears chose not to listen
although my patience wanes.

Like the moon, I bide my time
and hold my tongue like she holds tides
until the waves break heavy overhead
but by then, no one blames the moon.

SAVE MY SANITY

On the days I am blessed with patience
my spirit tends to wane
I follow strings of conversations
having long lost the beginning
with no end in sight.

My head lingers in a mild ache
not quite breaking but not quite whole
my mind clings to its final threads
my soul fades with each new day
begging for a respite that never comes.

Not weekends, not vacations
not bedtime or naps
restore my peace or clarity of mind
I wait for the day I will find a way
to save my sanity.

WHY THE HATE?

Does the tone of my skin mean
I feel no pain?
Does it mean I feel a different sun?
Does scored skin not bleed the same?

Does my heart break in different places
whether I am woman or man?
Is my love less valuable?
Less still if there's no ring on my hand?

What if my God wears blue robes and yours green?
Am I not worthy of being seen?
Is my silent prayer not allowed to be heard
if it is not loud-spoken bible verse?

Will I be doomed to be cast
always in the role of the other?
When I too am somebody's mother
or father or sister or brother?

Are we not all idols and icons?
Somebody's tether?
Somebody's haven?
Their for worse or for better?

Why has hate marked us?
Why has difference shined?
In a world filled with people
we've let ignorance preside.

So, we pray and pay tithes to our wickedest sins
in the names of the gods we create
rather than seeking out common virtues
and banishing the hate.

OUTGROWING

I sought refuge in the arms of the gentry
whose friendship I craved, but
whose wolfish eyes sought only a prize in me.
A lamb, primed by naivety,
in need of a shepherd and not sharpened claws.
A fruit, growing forbidden and fresh,
in need of tending, not teeth.
I fell for sweet nothings and bitter endings
pretending to be all that was needed
for I needed to be seen
needed it like the air I breathe
until I suffocated and suffered
through many a broken heart as
my innocence broke my soul.

But I fall no more.
For now I am stronger, I have grown bold
I found worth in my own company
and value in my own voice.
I seek not the pleasantries
of those whose brightest bonfires
could not hold a candle to mine,
or those who cried at my fallen leaves
and refused to admire the expanse of my roots.
I have grown wise to the guise of charm
worn by those whose masks have become their faces
but whose fates are left at the mercy of
the gods so readily marked on their skins
yet barred from their hearts and minds.

DO I LIKE TO DRINK?

Little me would not be proud
of the big me sipping on the glass
that may have been a second or third
of the dark red liquid we once despised.

Little me would chastise my bigger shadow
as it clings to the goblet like a protective charm
from the pressures of life and social anxieties
it somehow brought upon itself.

Even now my tongue recoils
knowing deep down it loathes the taste
the sharp tang of liquor that brings up my lunch
for it knows I don't like to drink.

THE COST OF GETTING TO SLEEP

Do you, with your greying hair and tired eyes,
remember what it feels like…
to wonder if you'll make the rent?
to wonder if you'll pay the bills?
keep food in the fridge?
keep the lights on?

Even in the darkness,
all I think about is light.
Even on the summer nights,
I think about the heat.
Even as my belly's full,
I wonder if I'll eat.

Do you, with your stable jobs and savings,
ever question what it is…
to not be able to leave the house
because you haven't more to spend?
because you cannot be sure if
you'll make it to month's end?

Even on the worst of days
all dreams to you are sweet
because you never factor in
the cost of getting to sleep.

HOUSTON, WE HAVE A PROBLEM

Houston…
Houston…
Houston…
Houston…
Houston, are you there?

Houston, we were clear for takeoff
There it goes, the sky, the ground
We're on our way to other worlds
We won't look down, only forward
Eyes on the horizon that's leaving us behind.

Houston, can you hear me?
hear me?
hear me!
hear me…
hear? me?
…me?

What happens if the system's busted?
If I'm running out of air?
Houston, can you hear me?
Someone please pick up the phone.
Where did I go wrong, go wrong, go wrong?
I'm here, I'm here, I'm all alone.

Houston, can you hear me?
can you?
can you!
can you…
can?

I'm being battered by a different gravity
and falling from darker skies
my lifeline in tow but I'm towing all alone…

Houston, can you hear me?
hear me?
hear me…
hear, me here, me
here… here… hear me, here…
Houston? Are you there?

I wonder if I close my eyes
will I be safe at home?
Snuggled in the bed beside
the person I used to know?

Houston
Houston
Houston
Houston
Houston… we have a problem.

I'M TIRED

I'm tired of changing…
and changing…
and changing…

Because I'm not enough
Because I'm too much
Because I'm not there
Because I will cry
Because I must lie
Because I'm not her
Because she's not me

Don't you see?

I'm tired of changing…
and changing…
and changing…

I am the master of disguise
Seelie temptress swarmed by lies
Kingdom's head of broken bones
Leader of the no-man's throne
Hobo's mansion rimmed with light
Christmas carols on Halloween night
The master of the best disguise

Is that me?

I'm tired of changing…
and changing…

I am your object of desire
when I break my nose
and shatter my toes
and cut my edges
and curb my glow
and follow which way
the right wind blows

Only then can I be she.

I'm tired of changing…

I've lost too much of myself in the process.
I've followed the rules and coloured in the lines.
Because I needed to people-please.
I've battered myself to fit in moulds.
I've blurred the space between expectation and me.
To make sure I was all the things you need.
I've lost too much of myself in the process.

But I am tired of changing.

PROVENCE ROSE

Provence rosé, a delicate and pale pink wine, is as charming as a romantic poem. Like a rose in bloom, Provence rosé enchants with its light and refreshing aroma of fresh strawberries, raspberries, and peaches.

Provence rosé is a wine that is both easy-drinking and sophisticated, like a well-written poem that is both simple and profound. Its understated elegance makes it a perfect choice for a wide range of occasions, from a casual picnic with friends to a romantic dinner for two.

To fully enjoy the beauty of Provence rosé, serve it chilled at 8-10°C (46-50°F) and pair it with light dishes such as grilled fish, salads, or fresh cheese.

The poems in this section leave a pleasant taste on the tongue, comparable to the delicacy of their namesake Provence Rose.

BLOOM WHEN READY

no violent sun will cause the rose to bloom
no torrential rain will help the bougainvillea grow
no predator chase will make the prey faster
nor hunger the latter accelerate.

this flower will bloom when ready.

WINTER LOVES FIREPLACES

knowing of your love's embrace
i stare at the fireplace's dying embers
as the storm rages beyond my windows.

but i will fall asleep
in the gentle calm of the sofa, alone
blanket in the armrest's hand, waiting
for i need it not to keep warm.

RESPITE

there is a part of my soul
which seeks refuge
in all that is not made
but born of the sun and soil
which needs no tending but mends
the wilder parts of me.

ONE DAY I FELL

One day I fell…
the way autumn leaves
drift in the wanton breeze,
I fell,
the way the tired eye
relents to the lure of sleep,
I fell,
unhurried by the passage
of a time that was never mine,
only borrowed.

I suppose it might have been love.

PRINTER JAM

i rap my fingers
staring at the feeding tray
the printer's jammed—again.

COFFEE MACHINE TALKS

a shared look, a laugh
experiences that last
'til the coffee's brewed

COFFEE MACHINE TALKS

a shared look, a laugh
experiences that last
'til the coffee's brewed

ADULTING

turn up the heating
fend off the cold, i wish to
an empty wallet.

RULES

Rules to be followed
norms to be upheld, goodbye
creativity.

FIND YOUR COMFORT ON OTHER ISLES

I will not be your paradise for the blind
when I can be another's braille.

68

SET IT FREE

Freedom was the space I gave you
before I learned you preferred a different cage.

69

SET IT FREE

Freedom was the space I gave you
before I learned you preferred a different cage.

VINES AND ROOTS

the soil beneath my feet is laced
with salt and sorrow and still my roots grow.

the sun above my head is shining
stretching its light and so my spirit spreads.

my feet untethered walk the old paths
my ancestors wandered, curious but not lost.

my heart is open and unlocked
and i now meet the world, unbound.

my vines are wild and my roots are strong
expanding across this lifetime and the ones beyond.

I AM MY OWN BANK

I am no longer beholden to the teller
at the bank who stares down at me
as if I were still the child she once knew
who had not a penny to her name.
Now, I am my own bank.
Now, I am free.

DANCE IN FRONT OF THE MIRROR

a shake of my hips, the dip of my head
a flash from beneath the hem of my dress
a smile curls below reddened cheeks
loose hair flies as my arms swing high
the rhythm reaches my bones
dancing like this is a sign of joy
love for the only me i'll ever know.

11:11

you taught me to wish on the time
I'm not sure if you even remember
it's been years now since
we were just kids way back when
sat in the car and wishing on numbers
of which we had and still have no concept.

you may not remember
but I'll never forget
how you looked into my eyes
and wished for my smile
and taught me of your magic
as you hoped to know mine.

forgotten or not, i may never know
but one thing is certain and always will be
my mind drifts towards the time
watching the clock, counting the seconds
to make a wish each time it strikes
11:11.

YOU'LL NEVER KNOW

the contents of my heart are hidden
to all but those who know to read
the pages of my open book,
whose words are written in languages unknown
and whose ink will smudge if not handled with care.

i'd once tried to let them be known
make myself heard, wanting to be seen
but i wasn't fluent then
in the verses of love and other hearts,
and so i became the subject of mockery.

i wish my heart would simply find
the other who speaks my tongue
and whose rhythm follows my verse…
i'd hoped it was you, once upon a time,
but now i think you'll never know.

BORDEAUX

Like an epic poem, Bordeaux wines are full of character and depth, the best of which are known for their ability to age gracefully, developing greater complexity and nuance over time, like a poem that reveals new meanings with each reading. They are synonymous with elegance and sophistication and are coveted by connoisseurs around the world.

To fully appreciate Bordeaux, serve it at a cool room temperature of 16-18°C (60-64°F) and pair it with hearty and flavorful dishes, such as steak, lamb, or game.

The following poems, like their alcoholic counterpart, are complex, classic, and reveal new meanings with each reading.

YOUNG BLOOD

a younger me had fresher blood
that i lost in scrapes and bruises
carelessly as i'd not yet known
the way the world thirsts for
the freshest blood.

GROWN-UP SKIN

my grownup skin has now come in,
—thin—and feels like justification
where i'd never needed it before.

OLIVE BRANCHES AND FUNERAL PYRES

The war was waged.
By whom? I forgot.
The world burns around us.
The silence is suffocating.
The scorning rings out loud.

The war was waged, and still, we fight.

Only ashes of bridges remain.
Cell towers downed and dying.
On the outside there is quiet,
all quiet on the western front,
but the north and south collide.

The war was waged, and here, we stand.

My pleas fall on deaf ears,
but I know Death can hear.
He mocks me in the way you stare
through the tears in my eyes
I refuse to let fall.

I gave you olive branches
but you used them for my funeral pyre
and where I'd hoped to broker peace
you left me set to dust
awaiting a truce that will never come.

The war was waged. And I have lost.

THE SHELL OF WEALTH

The shell of wealth is a house on the hill
overlooking the bayside of the Caribbean isles,
the ones in mildly worn travel guides
of sterile doctors' waiting rooms.

The shell of wealth is white walls and marble floors
staged to perfection for the outside eyes
as the ones inside seek out the marks
that time leaves on happy homes.

The shell of wealth is perfect porcelain and
open shelves that catch the dust that falls
like snow from empty skies over barren lands
unmarked by even the smallest of paws.

The shell of wealth sits mostly finished
with walk-in showers that soak the floors,
varnished windows, untrimmed walls,
and balconies with broken rails.

The shell of wealth is panes upon panes of
un-curtained glass that act as television screens
to vacant rooms and hollow halls
painted in shades of grey.

The shell of wealth was once the dream, the goal,
the medal at the end of the race we were told to fight
to win, but what good is the gold if you hold it alone?
A vacant diner sung to by a tarnished gramophone.

The shell of wealth is just that—a shell.

THE PRETENDER

I give up. That's it, no more. I'm done.
I'm done, I say to the girl in the mirror,
the girl who shares my face
the one I no longer recognize.

Tears line her cheeks
veins burn on her eyes
and she's done with the lies,
she thinks as she sighs.

Let me see her,
the one I should be
I thought I was her,
but now I know I will never be.

I fought and I fought hard
against red flags and bad cards
I thought I could make it through to the end
but now I see it was all pretend.

I'm good at pretending,
pretending and playing pretend.

You think you're good?
Well, I know I'm better
can't you see, I am
the very best pretender.

I'll pretend 'til the cows come home,
I'll pretend 'til I'm all alone
like the broken clock on my shelf
and don't recognize myself…

Then I'll cry at the mess I've made,
at the broken girl in the mirror who
once held hands with the moon and laughed
as she danced circles around the sun.

I'll look at the me in the mirror that now is
and wonder how she came to be
when all she wanted was to be
loved and loved sincerely, truly.

But she couldn't love herself.

And now she is here, and she is me and I am her.
The girl in the mirror crying over
endings that will turn into new beginnings
that will begin and end and begin again.

No more pretending to like things I don't
for the sake of a smile in which I cannot partake.
No more putting up with the things I hate
or convincing my tears away when I am not okay.

I was the pretender because I did it better.
But I've pretended my life away.

WHEN IT ALL COMES OFF

at the end of the day
when it all comes off
i am no longer the worker bee
or the girl in the red dress
my painted face gets washed down the drain
the scars i hide beneath satin or silk
hit the bed open and exposed
the titles no longer matter
for the dark does not speak
but it watches as i sleep
for i am nothing more than a tomb
a mound of mind and matter
as are you, as are we all
unbound by the things
we think make us better
when it all comes off.

LIFE ADJACENT

is this life?
the buying of things you don't need
to pacify a society
whose approval you seek
but do not want
but are convinced you require
to live a decent life?

is this life?
the need to be something bigger
the constant climbing to higher heights
to be heard above the trees
and seen amongst the stars
when that which you seek
resides at ground level?

is this life?
can this be living?
or is it being seen to live?
is this the supposed dream?
is this what matters?
is this life? I'll ask again.
or is it something adjacent?

ALONE AND HAPPY

growing up to me has become synonymous with
distinguishing those with whom I am alone and happy
from those with whom I am happy and alone.

FULL MOON

i pray in secret to the queen of the night
fearing mockery from those whose eyes
will never reflect the full moon.

THE QUESTION OF REINCARNATION

i wonder if this is the game i've chosen
and why should a soul like mine see fit
to choose the pendulum of emotions
that plague me in waking and sleep.

FIRST STAR I SEE TONIGHT

perhaps there is no such thing as fate
still i look to the heavens and wish
on the first star i find in the sky
for it has decided to guide my eyes
in a way i hope not coincidence.

FEMININE WILES

Let them say you are nothing more than
a face and a body, a losing cause.

Feminine wiles such as yours
cannot be understood but from within.

And they will soon see what it means
to have to do without.

A QUEEN AMONG MAIDS

I dare you, darling
take back your throne
reclaim your power
hold on to your own
your strength is far greater
than what they have known
you are more than a babe
show them now how you've grown.

WHEN I GO, I'M GONE

No longer do I stay where I am not wanted,
where I am not valued, where my worth is not seen.
No longer do I stay with those who cannot
reciprocate the care they've received from me.

I've put up and put up until I got fed up
and now I will no longer bend or break
to meet your 'good enough'
when yours has never been for me.

When I see my trying is tried out,
and I have grown tired of giving in,
I'll pack up the efforts and show you the same.
Maybe you'll learn, maybe you won't
but my fight is over before yours began.

You'll say I gave up because all you see is a tear
when my eyes have been fighting them for years
behind closed doors and from within empty halls
because I was afraid to let you see—to let you leave
but I'm handing in my resignation.

I'll tell you one last time that I'm tired of trying
and I'll hope for the change I've never seen
but don't come back after the fact
because all you'll do is hurt me more
because I'll know I was right all along
because I held value you could never see
because when I go, I'm gone.

TRUST THE PROCESS

Through the waves of emotion and pressures
and darkness, there is one guiding light I can find.
This is life.
For all those who are suffering with the getting up
and getting out and the going through and getting old.
This is love.
I have three words in which to seek solace.
Time heals all.
Three words we are often told but never hear.
Don't give up.
Three words that mean little.
You are strong.
Just keep going.
Until they mean everything.
You're almost there.
It's nearly done.
You're so close.
Do not quit.
Before meaning nothing at all.
You did it.
Sooner or later we all hear the applause.
My darling, trust the process.

GOODNIGHT, MY DEAR

Tomorrow is another day
relax, what's done is done
if you wake up next, then smile
for you can open your eyes
and if you do not rise again,
then be at peace tonight.

OTHER WORKS IN THIS COLLECTION...

If you enjoyed this book, please feel free to leave a review of it on your favourite sites. These reviews help small-time authors like me reach new audiences and are much appreciated!

Stay up to date on L. M. Sanguinette's new releases and giveaways by signing up for her mailing list or following her on social media. Find all the links at the page below:

https://linktr.ee/lmsanguinette/

Be on the lookout for more books coming soon!

ABOUT THE AUTHOR

L. M. Sanguinette was born on a small island in the Caribbean, where the palm trees watched over her like giants and the sea crept up to her feet to say hello. Ever since she was little, she surrounded herself with tales of fantasy and magic, hoping that one day, she too would be involved in a story like the ones that captured her imagination.

Years—and many rewatching's of Avatar: The Last Airbender—later, she is happily living in the worlds that her mind created, filling her bookshelves with more books than she will ever read and practising her own version of magic.

When she's not sitting at the computer, she can be found snorkelling near forgotten shores, twisting from silks that hang from the ceilings, or in one of the many hidden coffee shops of Madrid, conversing with the spirits of the old city and dreaming up new adventures.

OTHER WORKS

Welcome to Visanthe (#1, Legend of the Stones)
Visanthe in Ruin (#2, Legend of the Stones)
Visanthe Rising (#3, Legend of the Stones)

Of Arrows and Roses

The Days I Dream of Coffee
The Days I Dream of Chocolate
The Days I Dream of Chardonnay